Usborne
Cakes &
Cookies
for beginners

D1136781

Fiona Watt

Designed by Mary Cartwright
Illustrated by Kim Lane
Photography by Howard Allman
Recipes by Julia Kirby-Jones

Food preparation by Ricky Turner and Lizzie Harris
Cover illustration by Christyan Fox

Contents

Before you begin

Before you start to bake, read through the tips on these pages. Each recipe has a list of ingredients that you will need. Make sure that you have them all before you begin.

In most types of cooking, it doesn't matter if you change an ingredient or leave something out, but you can't do this when you are baking. It's also important that you measure things exactly and use the right size of tin, otherwise your cakes or cookies may not turn out correctly.

Take butter or margarine out of the fridge at least 30 minutes before you use it, unless the recipe says something different.

Always use medium-sized eggs unless the recipe says something else.

When you measure with a spoon, use a level spoonful, not a heaped one.

Equipment

If you are making a cake, use the size and shape of tin written in the recipe. If you use a different size, you may not have the correct amount of mixture.

Baking sheets

The cookies in this book are baked on baking sheets. Space out the uncooked cookies as they usually increase in size as they cook. When you use two baking sheets, put them into your oven one above the other. Cook the top one for the time the recipe says, then take it out. Move the bottom one up and cook until it's ready.

Your oven

Turn your oven on when the recipe tells you to, so that it heats up. If you have a fan oven, you'll need to lower the temperature or shorten the cooking time. Look in its instruction book to see what is recommended.

Preparing cake tins

You need to grease a cake tin or baking sheet to stop the cake or cookie mixture from sticking to it when it's cooked. In some recipes you also need to line the tin with baking parchment, greaseproof or rice paper, or sprinkle it with flour.

Grease the sides too.

To grease a tin, dip a paper towel into soft butter or margarine. Rub the towel over the bottom.

Which shelf?

Cook your cake or cookies on a shelf in the middle of your oven unless the recipe says something different. Always move the shelf to the middle before you turn on your oven. Don't leave an empty shelf above it.

Cooling

Make sure that you always wear oven gloves when you take anything out of the oven. Leave cakes or cookies in their tin or on the baking sheets for several minutes to cool. Then, put them on a wire rack to cool down completely.

To remove a cake from a loose-bottomed cake tin, put the tin onto a can. Press on the side of the tin so that it slides down.

To turn a cake out of a cake tin, put a wire rack on top of the tin. Turn it over so that the cake comes out.

Baking tips

These pages give you lots of cooking hints and tips that will help you with the recipes in this book. You'll also find other hints spread throughout the book.

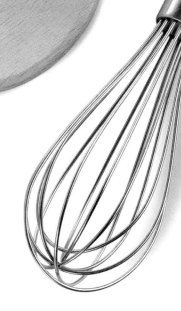

Breaking an egg

1. Crack the egg sharply on the rim of a cup or bowl. Push your thumbs into the crack in the shell and pull the sides apart.

2. Before you add an egg to a mixture, break the egg into a separate cup or bowl. It helps you to pick out any shell which may fall in.

Separating eggs

Don't let the yolk break.

Leave the yolk on the saucer.

Egg whites will not whisk if the bowl or whisk are greasy.

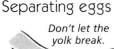

1. You will need a bowl and a saucer for this. Crack the egg on the side of the bowl, then pour it slowly onto the saucer.

2. Carefully put an egg cup over the yolk. Tip the saucer over the bowl so that the egg white dribbles into it.

If you are whisking the egg whites, make sure that your bowl and whisk are clean and dry before you start (see page 29).

Beating eggs

Beat with the fork like this.

Beating a mixture

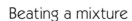

If you are beating eggs, you can use a fork instead of a whisk. Beat them until the white and yolk are mixed together.

1. Before you begin to beat a mixture, put your bowl on a damp dishcloth. This stops the bowl from slipping as you beat.

2. Stir the mixture briskly with a wooden spoon or a whisk. You are trying to get the mixture as smooth and creamy as you can.

Sifting

Shake the sieve until all the flour falls through.

Put a sieve over a bowl and pour the flour into it. If you sift wholemeal flour, tip any bran left in the sieve into the bowl.

Rubbing in

1. Cut the butter or margarine into small pieces and stir it into the flour. Stir until each piece is covered with flour.

Do this with clean, dry hands.

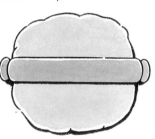

2. Rub the pieces with your fingertips. Lift the mixture and let it fall as you rub. Do this until it becomes like fine breadcrumbs.

Rolling out

1. Sprinkle a clean, dry work surface with a little flour. Put the dough onto it, then sprinkle a rolling pin with some flour.

2. Press the rolling pin onto the dough and roll it away from you. Turn the dough in a quarter turn and roll it again.

Shape the dough with your hands to keep it circular.

3. Carry on rolling and turning to make a circle, until you get the thickness of dough written in the recipe.

Melting chocolate

Stir the chocolate as it melts.

1. Heat about 2.5cm (1in) of water in a pan so that it is bubbling gently. Break the chocolate into a heatproof bowl.

2. Put on some oven gloves and lift the bowl into the pan. The heat from the water melts the chocolate gradually.

Testing a cake

At the end of the cooking time, test your cake to see if it is cooked. Press it in the middle. If it is cooked, it will feel firm and spring up.

Peanut butter cookies

Makes 12 cookies

50g (2oz) butter or margarine
75g (3oz) soft light brown sugar
100g (4oz) crunchy peanut butter
50g (2oz) self-raising flour
50g (2oz) rolled oats
1 medium egg

For the topping:
  50g (2oz) roasted,
    unsalted peanuts

1. Grease two baking sheets with butter or margarine. Turn the oven on to 170°C, 325°F, Gas mark 3, to heat up.

2. Put the margarine or butter into a large bowl. Add the sugar and peanut butter. Beat them until they are light and creamy.

3. Put a sieve over the bowl and sift the flour onto the mixture. Add the oats and stir well to mix everything together.

4. Press the mixture with your fingers, then fold it in half and press again. Do this again and again until it makes a soft dough.

5. Divide the mixture in half, then in quarters until you make 12 pieces. Squeeze each piece to make a small ball.

6. Put the balls onto the baking sheets, leaving plenty of space between them. Flatten them slightly with your hand.

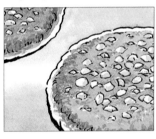

7. Break the egg into a small bowl and beat it well with a fork. Brush the top of each cookie with some beaten egg.

8. Cut the roasted peanuts into small pieces. Sprinkle them all over the top of each cookie. They will stick to the egg.

9. Bake the cookies for 15 minutes, until they are golden. Leave them on the trays to cool a little, then lift them onto a wire rack.

Corn flake crunch

Makes 8 pieces

200g (8oz) plain chocolate
3 tablespoons of golden
or maple syrup
50g (2oz) margarine
100g (4oz) corn flakes

a 20cm (8in) shallow tin

1. Grease the tin with a little butter or margarine on kitchen paper. Grease the inside well, but do not leave on too much butter.

2. Break the chocolate into a large pan. Add the syrup and margarine. Heat the pan gently, stirring all the time.

Lift the pieces out with a blunt knife or a pie slice.

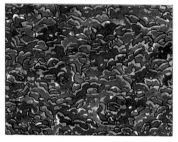

3. When the chocolate has melted, add the corn flakes and stir them well. Make sure that they are coated all over with chocolate.

4. Spoon the mixture into the tin. Gently smooth the top with the back of a spoon. Try not to crush the corn flakes.

5. Put the tin in a fridge for the chocolate to set. It will take about two hours. Use a sharp knife to cut it into eight pieces.

Marshmallow crispies

Makes 15 pieces

100g (4oz) wrapped toffees or slab toffee
100g (4oz) margarine
100g (4oz) marshmallows
100g (4oz) rice crispies

a shallow tin 27.5 x 17.5cm (11 x 7in)

1. Grease the tin (see page 3). If you are using a slab of toffee, put it in a plastic bag and break it up with a rolling pin.

They will take about 15 minutes to melt.

2. Put the toffee, margarine and marshmallows into a large pan. Melt them very gently over a low heat, stirring all the time.

3. When everything has melted and blended together, take the pan off the heat. Gently stir in the rice crispies.

4. Spoon the mixture into the tin and press it gently with the back of a metal spoon. Leave the mixture to set, then cut it up.

Chocolate chip cookies

Makes 12

100g (4oz) butter or margarine
100g (4oz) caster sugar
1 egg
half a teaspoon of vanilla essence
175g (6oz) plain flour
175g (6oz) chocolate chips

Use a wooden spoon.

1. Grease two large baking sheets with butter or margarine (see page 3). Turn your oven on to 180°C, 350°F, Gas mark 4.

2. Put the sugar and the butter or margarine into a large bowl. Beat it briskly until it is light and creamy (see page 4).

Press down on each cookie.

3. Break the egg into a small bowl and beat it well. Stir in the vanilla essence, then add the mixture to the large bowl.

4. Sift the flour into the large bowl and stir well to make a smooth mixture. Stir in 100g (4oz) of the chocolate chips.

5. Put a heaped tablespoon of the mixture onto a baking sheet. Use up the rest of the mixture to make eleven more cookies.

6. Flatten each cookie slightly with the back of a fork. Sprinkle the top of each one with some of the remaining chocolate chips.

7. Bake the cookies for 10-15 minutes. They should be pale golden brown and slightly soft in the middle.

8. Leave the cookies for a few minutes, then use a spatula or fish slice to lift them onto a wire rack. Leave them to cool.

Hazelnut cookies

Makes 15

150g (5oz) butter or margarine
100g (4oz) caster sugar
1 egg
175g (6oz) plain flour
25g (1oz) cocoa powder
75g (3oz) hazelnuts

You could press a whole hazelnut into the middle of the cookies before you bake them.

1. Follow steps 1-3 of the chocolate chip cookies, using the quantities shown above. You don't add any vanilla at step 3.

2. Sieve the flour and the cocoa powder into the bowl. Use a large spoon to stir it in well, until you get a smooth mixture.

Flatten them with the back of a spoon.

3. Put the hazelnuts onto a chopping board and cut them into pieces. Add them to the mixture and stir them in.

4. Put 15 heaped dessert spoonfuls of the mixture onto the baking sheets. Space them out. Flatten each one a little.

5. Bake the cookies for 10-15 minutes. They will darken. Leave them to cool a little, then lift them onto a wire rack.

11

Shortbread

Makes 8 pieces

150g (5oz) plain flour
25g (1oz) rice flour or ground rice
100g (4oz) butter, refrigerated
50g (2oz) caster sugar

a 20cm (8in) shallow tin

1. Turn your oven to 150°C, 300°F, Gas mark 2. Grease the inside of the tin with butter on a piece of kitchen paper.

2. Put a sieve over a large mixing bowl and pour the flour and the ground rice into it. Shake them into the bowl.

3. Cut the butter into small pieces and put them into the bowl. Mix them with a blunt knife to coat them with flour.

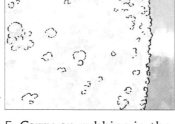

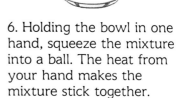

4. Rub the pieces of butter between your fingertips. Lift the mixture and let it fall back into the bowl as you rub (see page 5).

5. Carry on rubbing in the flour until the mixture looks like breadcrumbs. Stir in the caster sugar with a wooden spoon.

6. Holding the bowl in one hand, squeeze the mixture into a ball. The heat from your hand makes the mixture stick together.

Cut across it again, before lifting it out.

7. Press the mixture into the tin with your fingers, then use the back of a spoon to smooth the top and make it level.

8. Use the prongs of a fork to press a pattern around the edge. Then cut the mixture into eight equal pieces.

9. Bake it for 30 minutes, until it becomes golden. Leave the shortbread for five minutes before putting it on a wire rack.

Gingerbread biscuits

Makes about 20 biscuits

350g (12oz) plain flour
2 teaspoons of ground ginger
1 teaspoon of bicarbonate of soda
100g (4oz) butter or margarine
175g (6oz) soft light brown sugar
1 egg
4 tablespoons of golden syrup or
    maple syrup

large cookie cutters

1. Dip a paper towel in some margarine and rub it over two baking sheets. Turn on your oven to 190°C, 375°F, Gas mark 5.

Look at the tip for measuring syrup, below right.

2. Sift the flour, ginger and bicarbonate of soda into a mixing bowl. Cut the butter or margarine into chunks and add them.

3. Rub the butter or margarine into the flour with your fingers, until the mixture looks like fine breadcrumbs (see page 5).

4. Stir the sugar into the mixture. Break the egg into a small bowl. Add the syrup to the egg and beat them together well.

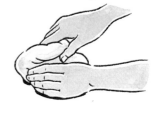

5. Stir the eggy mixture into the flour. Mix everything together with a metal spoon until it makes a dough.

6. Sprinkle a clean work surface with flour and put the dough onto it. Stretch the dough by pushing it away from you.

7. Fold the dough in half. Turn it and push it away from you again. Continue to push, turn and fold until the dough is smooth.

You can use any shape of cutter you like.

Spread the shapes out on the baking sheet.

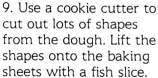

8. Cut the dough in half. Sprinkle a little more flour onto your work surface. Roll out the dough until it is about 5mm (¼in) thick.

9. Use a cookie cutter to cut out lots of shapes from the dough. Lift the shapes onto the baking sheets with a fish slice.

10. Roll out the other half of dough and cut shapes from it. Squeeze the scraps of dough to make a ball. Roll it out and cut more shapes.

Measuring syrup

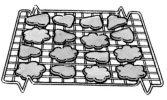

11. Put the biscuits on the baking sheets into your oven and bake them for 12-15 minutes. They will turn golden brown.

12. Leave the biscuits on the sheets for about five minutes. Then, lift them onto a wire rack. Leave them to cool.

Heat your spoon in hot water before you measure syrup. It makes it easier for the syrup to slide off.

Flapjacks

Makes 12

175g (6oz) margarine
175g (6oz) Demerara sugar
2 tablespoons of golden syrup
225g (8oz) rolled oats or porridge oats

a shallow 18 x 27cm (7 x 11in) tin

1. Put the tin on baking parchment or greaseproof paper and draw around it. Cut out the oblong just inside the line.

Cut the flapjacks while they are in the tin and still warm.

Grease the tin well.

2. Grease the bottom of the cake tin and put the paper in. Grease the paper. Turn on your oven to 160°C, 325°F, Gas mark 3.

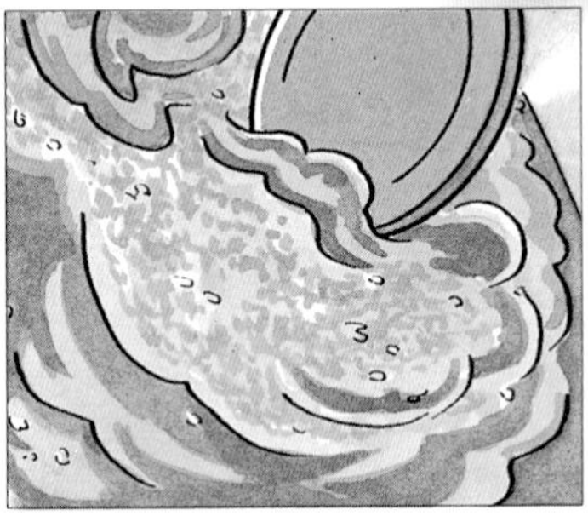

3. Put the margarine in a large pan with the sugar and syrup. Melt the margarine gently. Do not allow the mixture to boil.

4. Take the pan off the heat. Add the oats and stir them in really well so that they are covered in the margarine mixture.

5. Spoon the oats into the tin. Spread them all over the bottom, then smooth the top with the back of a metal spoon.

6. Put the tin on the middle shelf in your oven and bake the mixture for 25 minutes until the oats turn golden brown.

7. Take the tin out of the oven and leave it for ten minutes. Cut the mixture into pieces. Leave them in the tin until they are cold.

Chocolate refrigerator cake

Makes about 12 slices

100g (4oz) bar of plain chocolate,
Or, 100g (4oz) bar of white chocolate
100g (4oz) butter or margarine
5 tablespoons of golden syrup
225g (8oz) rich tea biscuits
2 tablespoons of chopped glacé cherries
2 tablespoons of raisins
2 tablespoons of chopped nuts

a 20cm (8in) round tin

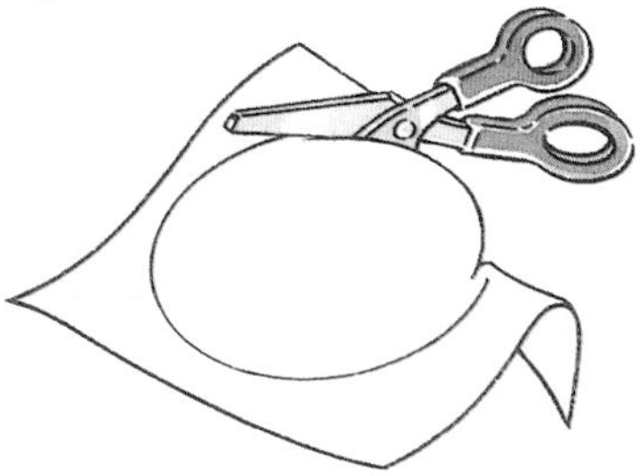

*Find out how to grease
a tin on page 3.*

*Use white
or plain
chocolate for
this recipe.*

1. Put your cake tin onto greaseproof paper and draw around it. Cut out the circle, just inside the line you have drawn.

2. Grease the tin. Put in the greaseproof paper circle you have cut out. Grease it again, on top of the paper circle.

3. Break the chocolate into pieces and put it in a saucepan. Add the butter or margarine and spoon in the syrup.

4. Put the pan over a low heat and let the mixture melt. Stir it occasionally. When the mixture has melted, turn off the heat.

5. Break the biscuits into pieces and put them into a bowl. Crush the pieces of biscuit finely with the end of a rolling pin.

6. Put the chopped glacé cherries, raisins and chopped nuts into the bowl. Add the mixture from the pan and stir well.

7. Spoon the mixture into the cake tin. Press it down really well, then smooth the top with the back of a metal spoon.

8. Put the tin into a fridge and leave it overnight. Turn the cake out and pull off the paper circle. Cut the cake into wedges.

Macaroons

Makes 12

3 large eggs (you only need the whites)
12 whole blanched almonds
75g (3oz) caster sugar
100g (4oz) ground almonds
25g (1oz) ground rice
a few drops of almond essence

Grease the top of the paper.

1. Turn your oven on to 150°C, 300°F, Gas mark 2. Cover the baking sheets with either rice paper or baking parchment.

If you don't have rice paper or baking parchment, cover the baking sheets with greaseproof paper. Grease the paper lightly.

Be careful not to break the yolk.

You don't need the yolks.

Lift them out with a teaspoon.

2. Break the egg on the side of a bowl. Hold it over a saucer and pull the sides apart. Let the egg fall gently onto a saucer.

3. Hold an egg cup over the egg yolk and tip the egg white into a large mixing bowl. Do the same with the other eggs.

4. Put the almonds into the egg white, then lift them out with a spoon. Put them on a plate and leave them on one side.

Make sure your whisk is clean and dry before you begin.

Use a metal spoon to fold the mixture (see the tip, page 47).

5. Whisk the egg whites (see the tip, page 29). Stop whisking when you get small points or 'peaks' when you lift your whisk.

6. Add the caster sugar, ground almonds, ground rice and almond essence. Fold the mixture over and over gently to mix them.

7. Put a heaped teaspoon of the mixture onto the paper on the baking sheet, and flatten it slightly with the back of the spoon.

The macaroons spread as they cook.

You can eat any rice paper left on the bottom.

8. Use up the rest of the mixture in the same way, leaving a space between each spoonful. Press an almond onto each one.

9. Bake the macaroons for 25-30 minutes, until they are pale golden brown. Leave them on the baking sheets for five minutes.

10. Lift the macaroons onto a wire rack to cool. If you have used rice paper, tear away the paper around each macaroon.

Fruity buns

Makes 12 buns

225g (8oz) self-raising flour
100g (4oz) butter or margarine
100g (4oz) caster sugar
1 medium egg
1 tablespoon of milk
50g (2oz) raspberry jam

You don't have to use raspberry jam, you could try different flavours, such as apricot or blackcurrant.

1. Turn your oven on to 200°C, 400°F, Gas mark 6. Grease two baking sheets and sprinkle them with flour. Shake them to spread the flour, then tip it off.

2. Put a sieve over a large bowl and shake the flour through it. Cut the butter or margarine into small chunks and add them to the flour.

3. Rub the chunks of butter or margarine into the flour with your fingers, until it looks like fine breadcrumbs (see page 5). Stir in the sugar.

4. Break the egg into a small bowl and add the milk. Whisk them together, then stir them into the mixture in the large bowl.

5. Sprinkle a clean work surface with some flour. Press the mixture together to make a firm ball, then put it onto your work surface.

Don't try to eat them while they are hot. The jam could burn you.

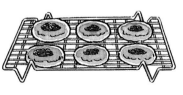

6. Cut the ball in half. Then, cut each half into three pieces. Cut each of the pieces in half. You should end up with 12 even-sized pieces.

7. Squeeze each piece into a round shape and spread them out on the baking sheets. Make a dent in each bun and fill it with a teaspoon of jam.

8. Bake the buns for ten minutes. They will rise and turn golden brown. Lift each one onto a wire rack and leave them to cool before eating them.

Chocolate choux buns

Makes about 18 buns

150ml (¼ pint) cold water
1 teaspoon caster sugar
50g (2oz) butter
60g (2½oz) plain flour
2 eggs

For the filling:
250ml (½ pint) double cream

For the icing:
225g (8oz) plain chocolate

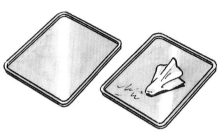  

1. Turn on your oven to 200°C, 400°F, Gas mark 6. Dip a paper towel in some margarine and rub it over two baking sheets.

2. Turn on the cold tap and hold each baking sheet under it. Shake them well to get rid of all the drops of water.

3. Put a sieve over a bowl and pour in the flour. Sift the flour into the bowl. Put this on one side. You'll need it later.

Beat the mixture quickly to mix in all the flour.

4. Put the water, sugar and butter into a large saucepan. Place the pan over a medium heat to melt the butter.

5. As soon as the butter has melted, turn up the heat and bring the mixture to the boil. Then, turn off the heat.

6. Immediately, shoot the flour into the pan in one go, and start to beat the mixture really well with a wooden spoon.

7. Keep beating the mixture until it makes a ball of smooth paste which leaves the sides of the pan clean.

8. Break the eggs into a small bowl and beat them. Add them, a little at a time, beating the mixture each time you add some.

9. Put teaspoonfuls of the mixture onto the baking sheets. Make sure that they are spaced out. They will spread as they cook.

Slit the buns to allow the hot air inside to escape.

10. Bake them for 25-30 minutes, until they are golden brown. Make a slit in each one and leave them on a rack to cool.

11. Whisk the cream until it is stiff. Cut the buns in half. Fill them with a teaspoon of cream, then press them together again.

12. Break the chocolate into chunks and let it melt in a bowl over a saucepan of hot water (see page 5).

13. Using a teaspoon, carefully coat the top of each bun with the melted chocolate. Leave the chocolate to harden.

Scones

Makes 16 scones

225g (8oz) self-raising flour
1 level teaspoon of baking powder
a pinch of salt
50g (2oz) butter or margarine
25g (1oz) caster sugar
125ml (¼ pint) milk
extra milk for brushing

6cm or 7cm (2½in) scone cutter

You can also make fruit scones by adding 50g (2oz) of sultanas, chopped glacé cherries or chopped dates, with the sugar at step 3.

Hold the sieve up above the bowl.

1. Turn your oven on to heat up to 230°C, 450°F, Gas mark 8. Grease two baking sheets with butter or margarine.

2. Sift the flour, baking powder and salt into a bowl. Cut the butter or margarine into small pieces and add them to the flour.

Use your fingertips.

3. Rub the butter or margarine into the flour until the mixture looks like fine breadcrumbs. Add the sugar and milk.

4. Use a blunt knife to mix everything to make a soft dough. Then, press and mould it with your fingers until it's smooth.

5. Sprinkle an area of your work surface with flour and put the dough onto it. Roll it out until the dough is about 1cm (½in) thick.

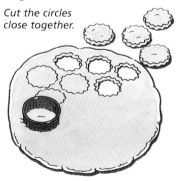

Cut the circles close together.

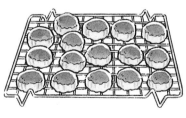

6. Cut circles from the dough with the cutter. Squeeze the scraps into a ball and roll them out again. Cut more circles.

7. Put the circles onto the baking sheets, leaving quite a lot of space between each one. Brush the tops with a little milk.

8. Bake the scones for 7-10 minutes on the top shelf of the oven. They will rise and turn golden. Lift them onto a wire rack to cool.

Baked cheesecake squares

Makes 15 squares

225g (8oz) plain flour
100g (4oz) butter
1 tablespoon of caster sugar
2 tablespoons of water

an 18 x 27 x 2.5cm (7 x 11 x 1in) tin

For the filling: 150ml (¼ pint) sour cream
225g (8oz) curd cheese, ricotta cheese
  or quark
50g (2oz) caster sugar
a lemon
3 eggs
50g (2oz) raisins

Rub in the butter until it looks like breadcrumbs.

1. Draw around the tray on baking parchment or greaseproof paper. Cut out the shape. Grease the tray and put the paper into it.

2. Turn your oven on to 200°C, 400°F, Gas mark 6. Sift the flour. Cut the butter into pieces and rub it in (see page 5).

3. Stir in the sugar. Add the water and mix to make a soft dough. Mix it until the mixture leaves the side of the bowl clean.

Beat the mixture until smooth.

4. Put the dough into the tray and press it with your fingers to cover the bottom of the tray. Press it right into the corners.

5. Prick the dough all over with a fork. Bake it for 10 minutes until it is golden. Turn the oven down to 160°C, 325°F, Gas mark 3.

6. Put the sour cream, cheese and caster sugar into a bowl. Grate the yellow rind off the lemon and add it. Beat the mixture well.

Turn the mixture over and over.

7. Separate the eggs (see page 4). Put the whites into a medium-sized bowl. Add the yolks to the mixture and beat it again.

8. Whisk the egg whites until they are stiff (see right). Fold them gently into the mixture with a metal spoon (see page 39).

9. Sprinkle the raisins over the dough and pour the eggy mixture on top. Bake for 45-50 minutes until it is golden brown.

Whisking egg whites

1. Separate the egg whites from their yolks and put them into a clean, dry bowl. Make sure that no yolk gets into the bowl.

2. Hold the bowl tightly in one hand and twist the whisk around and around. The egg will begin to go white and frothy.

3. Carry on whisking until the whites get stiff and you get points or 'peaks' forming on the top when you lift up the whisk.

Chocolate brownies

Makes 15

175g (6oz) margarine
350g (12oz) caster sugar
1 teaspoon of vanilla essence
3 eggs
100g (4oz) plain flour
1 level teaspoon of baking powder
75g (3oz) cocoa
175g (6oz) walnuts or pecan nuts

an oblong tin,
   22 x 30 x 2.5cm (9 x 12 x 1in)

1. Put your cake tin on a piece of greaseproof paper or baking parchment. Draw around it and cut out the shape.

2. Grease the tin. Lay the paper in the tin and grease the top of it. Turn the oven on to 180°C, 350°F, Gas mark 4.

3. Put the margarine into a pan and melt it over a low heat. Pour it into a large mixing bowl, then add the sugar and vanilla essence.

Beat the mixture each time you add some egg.

4. Break the eggs into a small bowl and beat them. Add them to the large bowl, a little at a time. Beat them in well.

5. Sift the flour into the bowl and add the baking powder and the cocoa. Stir everything together so that it is mixed well.

6. Put the nuts onto a chopping board and cut them into small pieces. Add them to the mixture and stir it well again.

7. Pour the mixture into the cake tin and smooth the top with the back of a spoon. Bake it for about 40 minutes.

8. The brownies are ready when they have risen and have formed a crust on top. They should still be soft in the middle.

Use a fish slice to lift them.

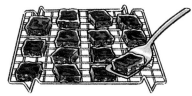

9. Leave the brownies in the tin for five minutes, then cut them into 15 squares. Leave them on a wire rack to cool.

Pecan squares

Makes 12 squares

For the base: 175g (6oz) butter or margarine
75g (3oz) icing sugar
225g (8oz) plain flour

For the topping: 75g (3oz) butter or margarine
2 tablespoons of golden or maple syrup
2 tablespoons of milk
1 teaspoon of vanilla essence
50g (2oz) soft brown sugar
2 eggs
100g (4oz) pecan nuts

an oblong tin, 18 x 27 x 2.5cm (7 x 11 x 1in)

1. Put the tin onto a piece of greaseproof paper or baking parchment. Draw around it and cut out the shape you have drawn.

2. Grease the tin. Put the paper into the bottom of the tin and press it down. Turn the oven on to 180°C, 350°F, Gas mark 4.

3. For the base, put the butter or margarine into a mixing bowl. Add the sugar and beat it until it is light and creamy.

4. Sift the flour into the bowl and stir it in well. Sprinkle flour onto a clean work surface and put the mixture onto it.

5. Press the mixture with your fingers, fold it in half, then press again. Do this again and again for about a minute.

6. Use the back of a spoon to press the mixture over the bottom of the tin. Bake it for about 15 minutes or until it is golden brown.

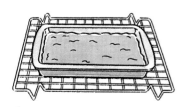  

7. When the base has cooked, leave it in the tin, but put it on a wire rack to cool. Begin to make the topping while it cools.

8. Put the butter or margarine into a pan and melt it over a low heat. Stir in the syrup, sugar, milk and vanilla essence.

9. Break the eggs into a small bowl and beat them well. Take the pan off the heat and stir the beaten eggs into the mixture.

10. Pour the topping onto the base. Sprinkle the pecan nuts evenly over the topping and bake it for about 25 minutes.

11. The topping will turn dark golden brown, but it should be slightly gooey in the middle. Leave it to cool in the tin.

12. When it has cooled, cut it into 12 squares, by making two cuts lengthways along the tin, then three cuts across.

Banana and nut slices

Makes 9 slices

100g (4oz) butter or margarine
100g (4oz) soft light brown sugar
2 eggs
2 bananas
100g (4oz) self-raising flour
1 teaspoon of baking powder
100g (4oz) chopped nuts

a 20cm (8in) square cake tin

1. Grease your cake tin with butter or margarine. Carefully follow the instructions on page 35 for lining your cake tin.

2. Turn on your oven to 190°C, 375°F, Gas mark 5. Put the butter or margarine into a mixing bowl. Add the sugar.

3. Use a wooden spoon to beat the butter or margarine and the sugar, until they are very smooth and creamy.

Greasing & lining a tin

4. Carefully break the eggs into a small bowl. Beat them with a whisk or a fork until they are mixed well (see page 4).

5. Add the beaten egg to the creamy mixture, a little at a time. Each time you add some egg, beat it into the mixture.

Put the tin on a piece of baking parchment or greaseproof paper which is larger than the tin.

6. Peel the bananas. Cut them into chunks, then put them into a bowl. Mash them well with the back of a fork.

7. Stir the mashed banana into the creamy mixture. Put a sieve over the bowl and sift the flour and baking powder into it.

Use a pencil to draw around the tin, as close to the bottom as you can. Lift the tin off.

8. Use a metal spoon to stir the flour into the mixture. Do this by turning the mixture over slowly with the spoon.

9. Spoon the mixture into your cake tin. Sprinkle the top with the chopped nuts and bake it for about 20-25 minutes.

Cut in from the edge to each corner of the square. Fold in each side along its pencil line.

10. Press lightly on the top of the cake to test it. It should spring back up. Leave it to cool in the tin for five minutes.

11. Hold the greaseproof paper and lift the cake out of the tin. Leave it on a wire rack to cool, then cut it into slices.

Grease the tin. Fit the paper into the tin. Trim off any extra paper, just above the tin.

Simple sponge cakes

Makes 18 squares. Ice the cakes with sugar icing or butter cream icing.

For the squares: 275g (10oz) self-raising flour
225g (8oz) soft margarine
4 tablespoons of milk
1 level teaspoon of baking powder
225g (8oz) caster sugar
2-3 drops of vanilla essence
4 eggs

For sugar icing: 225g (8oz) icing sugar
about 2 tablespoons of water

For butter cream icing:
75g (3oz) butter, softened
150g (6oz) icing sugar
1 teaspoon of vanilla essence

For decorating: small sweets

a 33 x 25cm (13 x 10in) roasting tin

Find out about greasing on page 3.

Use a wooden spoon.

1. Grease the tin. Draw around it on baking parchment or greaseproof paper. Cut out the shape and put it in the tin.

2. Turn the oven on to 180°C, 350°F, Gas mark 4. Put a sieve over a large mixing bowl and sift the flour through it.

3. Add the margarine, milk, baking powder, sugar and vanilla. Break the eggs into a small bowl, then add them too. Beat everything well.

Leave the cake in the tin to cool.

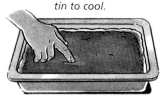

4. Scrape the mixture into the tin and smooth the top. Bake it for 40-45 minutes, until the cake springs up when you press the middle.

5. Make the icing when the cake has cooled completely. For sugar icing: sift the icing sugar into a bowl. Add a little water and stir.

Add some more water and stir it again. Continue to do this until the icing coats the back of the spoon and dribbles off it.

For butter cream icing: beat the butter in a bowl until it is creamy. Sift in the icing sugar. Add the vanilla and mix it well.

6. Lift the cake out of the tin, then spread the icing over it. Cut the cake into squares and decorate each piece before the icing sets.

Variations

Cherry and coconut: add 175g (6oz) chopped glacé cherries and 75g (3oz) desiccated coconut to the mixture at step 3.

Chocolate: add 2 tablespoons of cocoa powder to the mixture at step 3. Leave out the vanilla essence.

Lemon: grate the rind off two lemons and add it to the mixture at step 3. Leave out the vanilla essence.

Marble cake

Makes about 8 slices

225g (8oz) butter or margarine
225g (8oz) caster sugar
4 eggs
225g (8oz) self-raising flour

an orange
2 tablespoons of cocoa powder

a tin measuring 20.5 x 12.5 x 8cm
(8 x 5 x 3½ in)

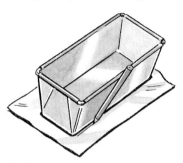

1. Put the tin onto some greaseproof paper or baking parchment and draw around the bottom. Cut out the shape.

2. Grease inside the tin, then put the paper into the bottom. Turn the oven on to 180°C, 350°F, Gas mark 4.

3. Put the butter or margarine and the sugar into a mixing bowl. Beat them until they are mixed well and creamy.

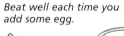

Beat well each time you add some egg.

4. Break the eggs into a small bowl and beat them. Add the beaten egg, a little at a time, to the creamy mixture.

5. Sift the flour into the bowl, then 'fold' it in with a metal spoon (see tip, right). Divide the mixture between two bowls.

Use the medium holes on your grater.

6. Grate the yellow rind off the orange. Take care not to grate any of the white part under the skin, as it tastes bitter.

7. Add the orange rind to one bowl and the cocoa powder to the other. Stir each bowl well, using separate spoons.

8. Put alternate spoonfuls of the mixture into the tin. Use a knife to make swirly patterns through the mixture. Smooth the top.

9. Bake the cake for an hour to an hour and 20 minutes. The cake should be well-risen and firm when you press it.

Folding in

You'll see the marble effect when you cut the cake.

10. Leave the cake in the tin for 10 minutes to cool, then turn it onto a wire rack. When it is cold, cut it into slices.

Use a metal spoon to cut through the middle of the mixture, then fold it over very gently. Do this again and again.

Carry on cutting and folding until the ingredients are mixed. Folding in keeps your mixture very light.

Layered lemon cake

Makes about 12 slices

a lemon
175g (6oz) self-raising flour
1 teaspoon of baking powder
3 eggs
175g (6oz) soft margarine
175g (6oz) caster sugar

For the filling:
2 eggs
75g (3oz) caster sugar

a lemon
50g (2oz) unsalted butter

For the icing:
a lemon
100g (4oz) icing sugar

two round 18cm (7in) tins

Heat your oven to 180°C, 350°F,
Gas mark 4.

Put a circle in the bottom of each tin.

Use the medium holes on the grater.

1. Turn on your oven. Draw around the tins on baking parchment or greaseproof paper. Cut out the circles. Grease the tins.

2. Grate the rind off a lemon, then cut the lemon in half. Twist each half on a lemon squeezer to get the juice from it.

3. Sift the flour and baking powder into a bowl. Break the eggs into a cup, then add them, along with the margarine and sugar.

Smooth the top with a spoon.

4. Beat everything in the bowl well, then stir in the lemon rind and juice. Divide the mixture between the two tins.

5. Bake the cakes for 25 minutes until they spring up when you press them in the middle. Leave them on a rack to cool.

6. While the cakes are cooling, make the filling. Break the eggs into a heatproof bowl and add the caster sugar.

Wear oven gloves.

It will take about 20 minutes.

7. Add the grated rind and juice of another lemon. Cut the butter into small pieces and add it to the bowl.

8. Put some water into a pan and turn on the heat so that the water is just bubbling. Put the bowl into the pan.

9. Stir the mixture from time to time as it thickens. Take it off the heat when it coats the back of your spoon. Leave it to cool.

Leave the cake on the rack.

A zester gives you long pieces of rind.

Press hard as you scrape.

Stir in the juice a little at a time.

10. Spread one cake with the filling. Put the other cake carefully on top. Don't worry if some of the filling oozes out.

11. Either grate some rind from the last lemon or scrape some off with a zester, if you have one. Keep it on one side.

12. Squeeze one half of the lemon. Sift the icing sugar. Stir the juice into the icing until it is like glue. Ice the cake. Sprinkle rind on top.

Apple cake

Makes about 12 slices

175g (6oz) wholemeal self-raising flour
175g (6oz) caster sugar
1 teaspoon of baking powder
3 eggs
175g (6oz) soft margarine

1 rounded teaspoon of ground cinnamon
50g (2oz) chopped nuts
1 cooking apple, about 250g (8oz)
Demerara sugar for sprinkling on top

a 20cm (8in) round, loose-bottomed
  cake tin

1. Put the cake tin onto some greaseproof paper or baking parchment. Draw around it and cut out the circle, just inside the line.

2. Grease the tin with some margarine, then put the paper into the bottom of it. Turn the oven on to 170°C, 325°F, Gas mark 3.

3. Sift the flour into a large bowl and tip in the grainy bits left in the bottom of your sieve. Add the caster sugar and baking powder.

This cake is delicious if you eat it while it is still slightly warm.

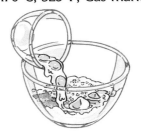

4. Break the eggs into a small bowl, then add them to the bowl along with the margarine, cinnamon and half of the nuts.

5. Use a wooden spoon to mix everything together really well. Spoon the mixture into the tin and smooth the top.

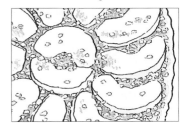

6. Peel the apple (see tip), then cut out the core. Cut the apple into thin slices. Lay the slices in circles on top, overlapping each one.

7. Sprinkle the apples with the remaining nuts and a tablespoon of Demerara sugar. Bake the cake for an hour, until it is firm.

Peeling apples

Put it on a wire rack to cool.

8. Leave the cake in the tin for ten minutes, before slipping off the ring of the tin and lifting the cake off the base. Leave it to cool.

Hold the apple in one hand. Scrape a vegetable peeler towards you again and again to remove the skin.

Apricot and orange loaf

Makes about 8 slices

100g (4oz) ready-to-eat dried apricots
an orange
100g (4oz) self-raising flour
100g (4oz) soft margarine
100g (4oz) light soft brown sugar
2 eggs

For the icing:
100g (4oz) icing sugar
2 tablespoons of orange juice

a loaf tin measuring 20.5 x 12.5 x 8cm
  (8 x 5 x 3½in)

1. Put the loaf tin onto baking parchment or greaseproof paper. Draw around the bottom of the tin and cut out the shape.

2. Grease the tin and put the paper into the bottom. Turn your oven on to heat up to 180°C, 350°F, Gas mark 4.

3. Use kitchen scissors to snip the dried apricots into small pieces. Cut them so that they fall into a large mixing bowl.

Use the medium holes on your grater.

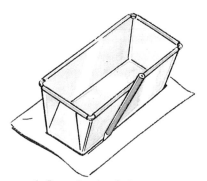

Tilt the bowl slightly as you beat.

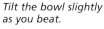

4. Grate the rind off the orange. Try not to grate any of the white pith underneath. Scrape the rind into the bowl.

5. Sift the flour into the bowl. Add the margarine and brown sugar. Break the eggs into a cup, then pour them in too.

6. Put the bowl onto a damp dishcloth. Beat the mixture firmly with a wooden spoon, until it is light and fluffy.

7. Scrape the mixture out of the bowl into the loaf tin. Smooth the top with the back of a spoon to make it level.

8. Bake the loaf for about 40 minutes, until it rises and turns golden. Leave it for a few minutes, then turn it onto a wire rack.

Pour on the icing when the loaf is cool.

9. Sieve the icing sugar into a bowl. Mix in some orange juice, a little at a time, until it is like runny glue. Pour it over the loaf.

Chocolate cobweb cake

Makes about 10 slices

2 rounded tablespoons of cocoa
4 tablespoons of hot water
225g (8oz) soft margarine
225g (8oz) caster sugar
4 eggs
175g (6oz) self-raising flour
1 level teaspoon of
baking powder
50g (2oz) ground rice

For the icing:
225g (8oz)
plain chocolate
100g (4oz) butter
50g (2oz)
white chocolate

two 20cm (8in)
round tins

*To make a different
pattern, do straight lines
across the cake and then
spread them with a
skewer.*

Make sure that the circles lie flat.

1. Draw around the tins on baking parchment or greaseproof paper. Cut out the circles. Grease the tins and put a circle in each one.

2. Turn your oven on to 180°C, 350°F, Gas mark 4. Put the cocoa into a small bowl. Add the hot water and mix until it's smooth.

3. Put the margarine, sugar, eggs, flour, baking powder and ground rice into a large bowl. Beat well, then stir in the cocoa mixture.

Smooth the top with a spoon.

4. Put half the mixture into each tin. Bake the cakes for 25 minutes until they rise. Turn them out onto a wire rack to cool.

5. For the icing, melt the plain chocolate in a bowl over a pan of hot water (see page 5). Cut up the butter and mix it in well.

6. Turn one cake flat-side up and spread on half of the icing. Put the other cake on top. Cover the top and sides with the rest of the icing.

Get someone to help you spoon in the chocolate.

7. Break the white chocolate into pieces and put it in a heatproof bowl. Melt it over a pan of hot water. Stir as it melts.

8. Leave the chocolate for five minutes, then take two small plastic bags and put one inside the other. Spoon in the chocolate.

9. Hold the bag over a plate and snip off a tiny corner. Be careful or the chocolate will start to run out immediately.

Tilt the bag between each circle to stop the chocolate running out.

10. Gently squeeze the bag as you draw a circle in the middle of the cake. Add more circles around it.

11. Drag a skewer or the tip of a knife from the centre out to the edge. Do this several times to make a cobweb pattern.

Index